Sig.ª Conte Alberto Pompei

ᵐᵃ (così io la supplico in sig. gratia) di
mio caratt. cancell. per riverenti lib:
devot; il qual per esser stata origini
re di V.E. M.ᵐᵃ alla qual bacio riverte le m.
Giovanna Pazzoni scrisse

FLORENTINES

A Pomegranate

STILL LIFE WITH BIRDS AND PEACHES

FLORENTINES
A Tuscan Feast

LORENZA DE' MEDICI
Illustrations by Giovanna Garzoni 1600–1670

RANDOM HOUSE, NEW YORK.

Anthology conceived, edited and designed by
© Jenny de Gex and David Fordham 1992

Foreword and recipes © 1992 by Lorenza de' Medici

Introduction copyright © 1992 by Jenny de Gex

Designed by David Fordham

Published in the United States by Random House, Inc., New York.

This work was originally published in Great Britain by
Pavilion Books Limited, London, in 1992.

Library of Congress Cataloging-in-Publication Data

de' Medici Stucchi, Lorenza.
Florentines: A Tuscan Feast/Lorenza de' Medici; illustrated by Giovanna Garzoni.
p. cm.
ISBN 0-679-41850-4
1. Cookery, Italian – Tuscan style. I. Title.
TX723.2.T86D39 1993
641.5945'5 – dc20 92-13767

Manufactured in Italy

2 4 6 8 9 7 5 3

First U.S. edition

Contents

List of Recipes

DECORATIVE LETTER G FROM THE LIBRO DELLA CANCELLERESCHE CORSIVE

Foreword

THE PORTRAIT OF FERDINANDO II DE' MEDICI HAS been housed in the drawing-room of my house in Milan since the death of my father, who left it to me in his will. It is the only portrait of a member of the family which my father succeeded in buying, after years of searching. He found it in France, where it had been exported goodness knows how long before. Apart from his impassioned search for family portraits, which brought him little but frustration, my father also had another hope. At a time when nobody, or almost nobody, had heard of Giovanna Garzoni, he began an intensive search for her temperas and miniatures, like those now on display at the Palazzo Pitti.

Unfortunately his hopes were never realised. Now, a few years after my father's death, scholarly research in Italy and America has brought the beauty of Garzoni's paintings to light once more. In writing this foreword, I am happy to reestablish the link between Garzoni and the Medici, as Giovanna was greatly protected by and carried out many commissions for my ancestors, including the Grand Duke Ferdinando II.

The Florentine Medici encouraged many of the world's greatest artists but there were others who flourished at their court. Many of these were women, yet Giovanna was one of the most accomplished. She was not merely an able craftswoman or a conscientious copyist, as you can see from the figurative qualities shown in this selection of her still-life arrangements. As a kind of tribute to these, I have added recipes reflecting the subjects painted; almost all are revisions of ancient recipes in vogue in the late Renaissance.

LORENZA DE' MEDICI, 1992.

HAZELNUTS, WITH AN APPLE AND A POD

12

Introduction

LIKE A RECIPE, THIS ANTHOLOGY IS COMPOSED OF several disparate ingredients. Foremost amongst these are the still-life paintings of Giovanna Garzoni. The second most important ingredient is Tuscan food, and who better to present this than Lorenza de' Medici, whose timeless recipes open the door to the world of her ancestors. The third ingredient is the Medici family, some of whose lavish marriage feasts or banquets are described with anecdotal examples of life at their court. The fourth ingredient is the city of Florence, whose turbulent, wealthy and powerful history during the earlier Renaissance influenced the entire world, as so many minds of genius generated new ideas in the arts, sciences and humanities. As fifth ingredient, descriptions by early travel writers, whose journals and diaries give an outsider's reactions to the countryside, food, customs and people of Italy. The final ingredients are the texts introducing each recipe, which are taken from *A Brief Account of the Fruit, Herbs and Vegetables of Italy* written in 1614, by Giacomo Castelvetro, whose encitement to eat more fruit and vegetables, is as relevant to a healthy diet now, as then.

The rediscovery of Giovanna Garzoni's work began with her inclusion in a classic exhibition of Italian still-life paintings in Naples in 1964. Subsequently, many studies and publications have brought knowledge of her scant biography and catalogue of work to the current level, culminating in publication of the first monograph by Gerardo Casale in 1991. Previously uncatalogued works have been identified, correctly attributed and confirmed with the Medicean inventories. It is the generosity of these experts' knowledge that has enabled us to compile this anthology.

Giovanna Garzoni left her native town of Ascoli, in the Marche, and worked under patronage in major cities, beginning in Venice, in 1625, during which time she also composed a volume of calligraphy (shown in our endpapers). By 1630 she was in Naples, at the court of the Spanish Duke of Alcalà, proved in correspondence with a famous Roman connoisseur, Cassiano del Pozzo. In 1632 she moved to Turin, and worked for five years at the court of the Duke of Savoy, mainly painting portraits. Although she enjoyed a considerable reputation in her lifetime, she is rarely mentioned by contemporary sources. But she was especially appreciated in Florence, where she stayed in the 1640's, although it is possible she made a previous visit, as the style she developed derives from that of Jacopo Ligozzi, the sixteenth century master of natural history painting.

The Florentine years were some of her most productive, as documented in a surviving account book. She worked as court miniaturist to the Grand Duke Ferdinando II, his wife the Grand Duchess Vittoria della Rovere, his brothers Cardinal Giovan Carlo, and Prince Leopoldo. She painted portraits, copied old masters, and created original and very stylised still-life compositions, placing subjects against neutral backgrounds, with odd manipulations of scale and perspective. The definition of miniature painting referred not to size but to the technique, similar to illuminated manuscripts, of using tempera on parchment or vellum. This creates an almost three-dimensional effect. Her freshness of style comes from a delicate balance between natural science illustration and her own gift for decorative design. It is possible she sometimes used a convex mirror, as these were a standard aid in every painter's studio.

After 1654, her name appears frequently in the records of the Accademia di San Luca, an academy for the study of the fine arts in Rome. Whilst there, she continued to paint for her Medici patrons until her death in 1670, ending her days as a Cappucin tertiary at the Accademia, to whom she bequeathed all her own papers, her *libro delle miniature* which was a form of sample book for potential customers, and her considerable art collection.

Lorenza de' Medici's recipes are an embodiment of the spirit of Tuscan cooking, for no other region of Italy holds such an emotive appeal to the British, who fall in love with the rich treasures of Florence and the unparalleled natural beauty of Tuscany, with its fine blend of the wild and civilised. The heady combination of colours, smells and tastes cannot fail to leave a lasting impression. The name derives from its ancient Etruscan origin (*Etruria*). From as early as the eighth century B.C. the Etruscans were known for their simple enjoyment of life: surviving frescoes show people drinking, fishing, cooking steaks or chickens opened flat over a fire, the latter method still in use today. Herbs are especially important to Tuscan cooking, particularly rosemary, sage and basil. Olive oil is used for frying, and a simple method of grilling over chestnut or vine embers produces unique flavour.

Despite the excesses of Renaissance court banquets, Tuscan food remained rustic, becoming renowned for its freshness and lightness, for the Tuscans like their food fresh from the land. The Medici were keen innovators in gardening, instructing their ambassadors to bring back plants or seeds from foreign climes and introduce them to Tuscany. Garzoni's paintings bear witness to this growing interest in fruit and vegetables, whilst stimulating our taste buds. Noble families such as the Medici owned large country estates: the painting of *The Old Man of Artimino* reflects this, showing natural home-grown produce, from Artimino which was just one of their many properties. Others with more modest estates or smallholdings could nonetheless benefit from the fertile hillsides, providing the finest of olive oil, grapes for wine or eating, wheat, fresh fruit and vegetables, and pastures dotted

VIEW OF FLORENCE

with sheep and cattle producing the finest beef in Italy, reinforced by the renowned *bistecca alla fiorentina*.

It is claimed that Catherine de' Medici changed the course of French cuisine, by introducing Italian cooks to the French court. Pastry-making had just arrived in Florence, and this certainly had an influence, as did sorbets and ice cream.

The Medici line had seen great glory but was in decline by the time Garzoni reached Florence. Harold Acton sums up the family history thus: "The facts are too familiar – that they were originally bankers by profession who gently, without military resources or experience of war, established a despotism which, with two interruptions, lasted for three centuries; that they established it when Florence was the intellectual capital of Europe; provided Rome with two great Popes, France with two great Queens; and that Medicean blood has flowed into every great dynasty in Europe." Commerce flourished, as did art and science, under their patronage: their collections contained works by Botticelli, Michaelangelo, Mantegna, Raphael, Titian and countless other masters.

Lorenzo 'Il Magnifico' dominated the fifteenth century, Cosimo I the sixteenth, becoming the first Grand Duke in 1574, thus uniting the previously warring city states of Florence, Siena and Pisa. Cosimo emulated 'Il Magnifico' in his patronage of the arts, financing his enterprises by taxation rather than banking.

Cosimo's son, Ferdinando I created some of the most astonishing theatrical spectacles ever seen in Florence, notably in 1589 for his marriage to Christine of Lorraine 'an unheard-of marvel and wonder'. This was only slightly over-shadowed by the suspicion of his having poisoned his brother. Festivities lasted for three weeks culminating in the inter-mezzi, a combination of music, drama and spectacle, and landmark in the origins of opera.

Nothing was too extravagant: in 1600, for the marriage feast of Henri IV of Navarre and Marie de' Medici, the sculptor Giovanni de Bologna modelled various figures and statues in confectionery and sugar, moved by hidden mechanisms. An effigy of the King of France, mounted upon a charger, trotted down the table, at an allegorical banquet in the Salone del Cinquecento of the Palazzo Vecchio, the splendour of which astonished even the French.

Fête after fête continued, with a *palio* (horse race), tournaments, musical entertainments until the departure of the bride. In 1608 there were similar entertainments for Cosimo II's marriage to Maria Maddalena of Austria, but in 1621, he died of consumption, succeeded by his 11 year old son, the future Ferdinando II, who married the daughter of the Duke of Urbino, Vittoria della Rovere, in 1634. Many of Garzoni's paintings now in the Pitti Palace came from their villa at Poggio Imperiale. It is this couple, together with Ferdinando's brothers Cardinal Giovan Carlo, known for his 'most unclerical orgies', and Prince Leopoldo, that we have to thank for the survival of the delicate works of Garzoni. Garzoni's correspondence with Giovan Carlo and Leopoldo shows just how much she was dependent upon them. Cosimo III was alas not a credit to his family, nor was his son, and the power of the dynasty gradually declined and faded.

Florence needs little introduction: her history is enshrined for posterity in the beauty of her buildings and treasures. Academies of learning were founded, as were the 'Arti' or Guilds, representing various trades be they connected with wool, silk, fur, olive oil, or building.

The Florentines, although known pejoratively by other Italians as '*mangia fagioli*' or eaters of beans, always enjoyed a particular habit of eating and chatting together at long tables, and even today this continues in some *trattorie*.

Although some traditional fêtes and ceremonies still take place, others are preserved only in the writings of contemporary or nineteenth-century historians, or early travellers.

For the final ingredient, we have the witty pen of Giacomo Castelvetro to thank. He came to England in the 1580's, a Protestant fleeing the Inquisition, enjoying the literary world of Elizabethan London. In 1592 he was Italian tutor to James VI of Scotland. After his wife's death he went to the courts of Denmark and Sweden, there developing a passion for gardening with Duke (later King) Charles. Returning to Italy, he settled in Venice, returning to England in 1613 after imprisonment for anti-papal activities.

His book, written in 1614, was an attempt to persuade the English to eat more fruit and vegetables. He achieves this with seasonal accounts of the produce of his beloved Italy, extolling the virtues of fresh, simply prepared, vegetables, which today is perfectly in tune with current thinking on healthy diets.

Making the link between Garzoni and Castelvetro, Jane Grigson wrote: "The visual embodiment of the *Brieve racconto* may be seen in Giovanna Garzoni's miniature painting. Garzoni's life overlapped Castelvetro's. She too travelled about, looking for work, with Paris as her furthest destination. When Garzoni at last settled for some years in Florence, she was able to depict fruit and vegetables – and their attendant insects – with that fine sympathy and joy that Castelvetro showed in his writing. The sensuousness is there, not in heavy contrasts of chiaroscuro, but in translucent colours and clarity of form. It is the kind of poetic, almost humorous clarity that we do not much pursue in the north."

As a footnote, from a humble northerner, I was lucky to experience that translucence first-hand, by handling many of the Garzoni miniatures, both in Florence and Rome, thus very aware of their unique quality. One stepped instantly into a world of sunshine, the more surprising, as outside, it was December, and patches of ice lay on the vast expanse of the Piazza della Signoria.

JENNY DE GEX, 1992.

Spuma di Foie Gras in Salsa di Melone

MOUSSE OF FOIE GRAS WITH MELON SAUCE

"As June comes to an end the melons start to be good. I take my hat off to this fruit; it is my favourite for no other reason than its marvellous sweet scent, the most wonderful perfume in the world. Believe me, none of the foreign melons have the fragrance that ours have, not even those of Provence or Spain, for all the care and trouble they take to produce even just a few fairly good varieties."

450 g/1 lb pâté de foie gras, sliced thinly
450 g/1 lb ricotta cheese
90 ml/3 fl oz Vin Santo (or port or Madeira)
1 ½ tsp powdered unflavoured gelatine
600 g/1 ¼ lb orange-fleshed melon, such as cantaloupe,
charentais, etc.
3 tbsp port

PLACE THE PÂTÉ DE FOIE GRAS AND RICOTTA IN A food processor fitted with metal blades. Blend until smooth. Heat the Vin Santo in a saucepan over low heat, then remove from the heat and sprinkle over the gelatine.

Stir to dissolve, then add to the foie gras mixture. Mix thoroughly, pulsing the machine on and off. Alternatively, put the pâté and ricotta through a food mill into a bowl and add the dissolved gelatine.

Wet a 17.5 cm/7 inch mould with cold water and pour in the foie gras mixture. Chill for about 5 hours (it can be left in the refrigerator for up to 12 hours).

Peel the melon, remove the seeds and filaments and place the flesh in a processor fitted with metal blades. Blend until the texture is smooth and creamy, then mix in the port.

To remove the mousse from the mould, dip the base of the container in a saucepan full of boiling water for 5 seconds, set an upturned plate on top and turn them over, holding them tightly together. If the mousse still sticks, re-immerse in the water. Pour the melon sauce around and serve.

A Melon and a Slice of Watermelon

19

CHERRIES, STRAWBERRIES AND PEAS

Of Fruit and Vegetables
by
Giacomo CASTELVETRO

BRIEVE RACCONTO DI TUTTE LE RADICI, DI TUTTE L'HERBE ET DI
TUTTI FRUTTI, CHE CRUDI O COTTO IN ITALIA SI MANGIANO
(A BRIEF ACCOUNT OF THE FRUIT, HERBS AND VEGETABLES OF
ITALY)

WHEN YOU CONSIDER THE REASONS, IT IS HARDLY surprising that we Italians eat such a profusion of fruit and vegetables, some of them quite unknown and unappreciated elsewhere. Firstly, Italy, though beautiful, is not as plentifully endowed as France or this fertile island with meat, so we make it our business to devise other ways of feeding our excessive population.

The other equally powerful reason is that the heat, which persists for almost nine months of the year, has the effect of making meat seem quite repellent, especially beef, which in such a temperature one can hardly bear to look at, let alone eat. Even mutton is not eaten much; for we keep the animals closed in stalls at night, not in the fields as you do, and this gives the meat a somewhat unpleasant taste.

This is why we prefer our fruit and vegetables, for they are refreshing, they do not thicken the blood and above all they revive the flagging appetite.

GIACOMO CASTELVETRO, 1614.

A Dish of Medlars and a Rose, with Almonds

22

Crema di Cipolle alle Mandorle

ONION AND ALMOND SOUP

"GREEN ALMONDS ARE GOOD ABOUT NOW [*summer*], or even earlier, but are not in season long; they are much healthier than hazelnuts, and considered to be the noblest nut of all. Many people in Italy, especially in Tuscany, eat them green when the shell is still soft, or cook them like truffles."

6 medium red or yellow onions
4 tbsp extra virgin olive oil
1.5 litres/2 ½ pints/1 ½ quarts chicken stock
180 g/6 oz/1 cup blanched almonds, freshly ground in a blender
1 tsp ground cinnamon
1 tsp grated nutmeg
2 tbsp crushed amaretto biscuits (cookies)
salt and pepper

THIS IS A MODERN VERSION OF A VERY FAMOUS Renaissance soup, when instead of herbs food was seasoned with spices. I like to serve it in wintertime, followed by *Arista di maiale al finocchio*.

Peel the onions and slice them finely. In a large saucepan heat the olive oil, add the onions and sauté over low heat until translucent, about 10 minutes.

Add the stock and the almonds and allow to simmer for about 30 minutes.

Transfer the soup to a blender or food processor and purée. Add the cinnamon, nutmeg, amaretto, and salt and pepper to taste. Process until creamy.

Return the soup to the saucepan and bring to the boil. Pour the soup into a tureen and serve at once.

Of Their Manner of Eating
by
Fynes MORYSON

IN GENERALL THE ITALIANS, AND MORE SPECIALLY THE Florentines, are most neate at the Table, and in their Innes from morning to night the Tables are spread with white cloathes, strewed with flowers and figge leaves, with Ingestars or glasses of divers coloured wines set upon them, and delicate fruits, which would invite a Man to eat and drink, who otherwise hath no appetite, being all open to the sight of passengers as they ride by the high way, through their great unglased windowes. At the Table, they touch no meate with the hand, but with a forke of silver or other mettall, each man being served with his forke and spoone, and glasse to drinke. And as they serve small peeces of flesh, (not whole joints as with us), so these peeces are cut into small bits, to be taken up with the forke, and they seeth the flesh till it be very tender. In Summer time, they set a broad earthen vessel full of water upon the Table, wherein little glasses filled with wine doe swimme for coolenesse. They use no spits to roast flesh, but commonly stew the same in earthen pipkins, and they feed much upon little fishes and flesh cut and fried with oyle.

AN ITINERARY, FYNES MORYSON, 1605–17.

A Dish of Figs

25

Crema di Patate e Porri

CREAM OF POTATO AND LEEK SOUP

"I OFTEN REFLECT UPON THE VARIETY OF GOOD THINGS to eat which have been introduced into this noble country of yours over the past fifty years. The vast influx of so many refugees from the evils and cruelties of the Roman Inquisition has led to the introduction of delights previously considered inedible, worthless or even poisonous. Yet I am amazed that so few of these delicious and health-giving plants are being grown to be eaten."

600 g/1 ¼ lb leeks
30 g/1 oz/2 tbsp unsalted butter
1 tbsp extra virgin olive oil
120 ml/4 fl oz water
4 tbsp dry white wine
6 medium boiling potatoes
120 g/4 oz Gruyère or Emmental cheese, grated
600 ml/1 pint/2 ½ cups milk
600 ml/1 pint/2 ½ cups light meat stock
½ tbsp grated nutmeg
salt and pepper

REMOVE THE TOUGH GREEN LEAVES AND THE ROOTS from the leeks. Wash carefully and slice thinly. In a saucepan heat the butter and olive oil. Add the sliced leeks and cook gently on low heat for about 10 minutes, until translucent. Add the water and wine and leave to simmer over low heat for another 10 minutes.

Scrub the potatoes and cook them in their skins in boiling water until tender. Drain, then peel and slice the potatoes.

Purée the leeks with their cooking liquid, the sliced pota-toes and grated cheese in a blender or food processor. Transfer the purée to a clean saucepan. Stir in the milk and stock and bring to the boil. Season with the nutmeg and salt, pepper to taste and serve in individual bowls.

Onions can be used instead of leeks, and although they are strongly flavoured they make an excellent cream. For a dinner party I occasionally put three or four scampi or shrimp tails in the middle of each bowl. The scampi or shrimp should be tossed in a little hot oil for just a couple of minutes.

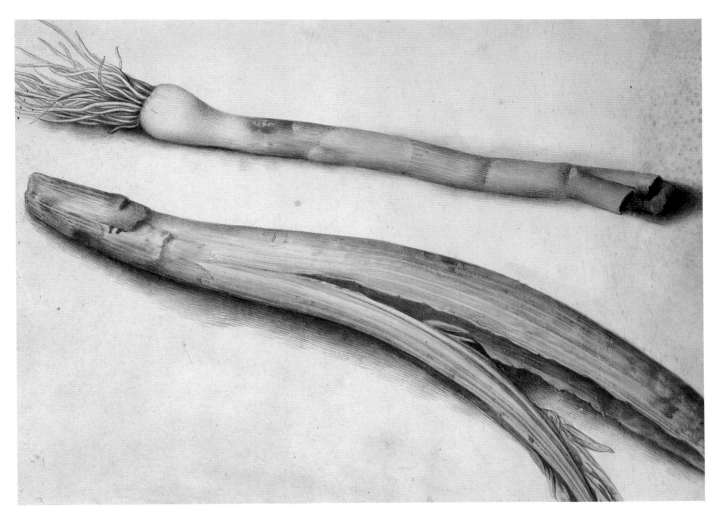

LEEK AND CARDOON

27

Passato di Spinaci alle Nocciole

CREAM OF SPINACH SOUP WITH HAZELNUTS

"HAZELNUTS ARE GOOD TO EAT both green and dried. We keep the dried ones for eating in winter and during Lent. Some people think they are indigestible, and bad for the catarrh, but then, as the proverb says:
Ogni cosa è sana al huomo sano.
Everything is wholesome to the healthy."

90 g/3 oz/¾ cup peeled hazelnuts
1.2 kg/2 ½ lb fresh spinach with stalks
30 g/1 oz/2 tbsp unsalted butter, at room temperature
30 g/1 oz/3 ½ tbsp flour
240 ml/8 fl oz milk
1.2 litres/2 pints/5 cups light chicken stock
1 tsp grated nutmeg
salt

Toast the peeled hazelnuts in a preheated 180°C/350°F/gas 4 oven for just a few minutes. Remove and chop coarsely.

Bring a large pan of salted water to the boil. Add the spinach, cover and cook until tender, about 3 minutes. Drain the spinach and refresh it in a bowl of ice-cold water, to prevent it losing colour.

Drain and squeeze out excess liquid. Put the spinach through a food mill or a sieve.

In a saucepan large enough to contain all the ingredients, melt the butter over moderate heat. Add the flour and stir until well blended. Using a wooden spoon, gradually stir in the milk and continue stirring until you have a smooth, thick sauce. Add the spinach, sprinkle with the nutmeg and stir well. Pour in the stock and blend well.

Allow the soup to simmer for about 5 minutes. Taste and add salt if necessary. Pour into a soup tureen, sprinkle with the chopped hazelnuts and serve at once.

A Dish with Plums, Hazelnuts, Jasmine and a Fly

Giovanna de' Medici's Marriage Feast
by
Guido BIAGI

GIOVANNA DE' MEDICI CAME TO HER WEDDING accompanied, as was the custom, by four cavaliers, chosen from among the elders of the city – Messer Manno Temperani, Messer Carlo Pandolfini, Messer Giovannozzo Pitti, and Messer Tommaso Soderini. There came to the wedding fifty gentlewomen richly dressed, and fifty gentle youths in beautiful costumes. The gaieties lasted from Sunday morning till Tuesday evening, and there were meals twice a day. Usually there were asked to each meal fifty persons, including relations, friends, and the chief citizens: so that at the first table there were, counting the women and girls of the house, trumpeters and pipers, about one hundred and seventy persons; at the second and third tables – the so-called low tables – there sat a large number of persons. At one meal they amounted to five hundred. The dishes, those prescribed by custom, were exquisite and abundant. On Sunday morning they had boiled capons and tongue, a roast of meat, and another of small chickens garnished with sugar and rosewater; in the evening, galantine, roast meat and chickens with fritters. Monday morning, *blancmanger*, boiled capons with sausages and roast chickens; in the evening the usual courses, with tarts of sugar and almonds. On Tuesday morning, roast meat and quails; in the evening the usual roast and galantine. At the refreshments there appeared twenty confectioners, who distributed a profusion of caramels made of pine-seed. The expenses of these banquets amounted to above 150,000 francs – an immense sum in those days. There had been bought 70 bushels of bread, 2,900 white loaves, 4,000 wafers, 50 barrels of sweet white wine, 1,500 couple of poultry, 1,500 eggs, 4 calves, 20 large basins of galantine; 12 *cataste* of wood were burnt in the kitchen fires. Verily it seemed the reign of abundance.

MEN AND MANNERS OF OLD FLORENCE, GUIDO BIAGI, 1909.

GIOSTRA DEI VENTI, 1608

TALL FRUIT BOWL WITH TWO EGGS, TWO PLUMS, BENEATH, TWO WALNUTS

32

Uova in Gelatina al Basilico

Poached Eggs in Basil Aspic

"'Sweet herbs' is the name our housewives give to a special mixture of parsley, spinach beets, mint, borage, marjoram, basil and thyme (but with more of the first two since the others are so strongly flavoured), which they wash and then chop very fine. We use this mixture to season many dishes, especially fresh broad beans."

1 tbsp white wine vinegar
salt
6 eggs, at room temperature
240 ml/8 fl oz light chicken stock
4 ½ tsp powdered unflavoured gelatine
3 tbsp finely chopped fresh basil
6 tbsp mayonnaise
6 tbsp finely grated Parmesan cheese
1 tbsp sweet paprika

In a wide shallow pan bring 5 cm/2 inches of water to a simmer. Stir in the vinegar and a pinch of salt.

Break each egg on to a saucer and gently slide it into the water. Spoon hot water over the eggs for 2 or 3 minutes. They are done when the whites are opaque and the yolks lightly set. Using a slotted spoon, transfer the eggs one by one to a bowl of cold water where they may be kept in the refrigerator for several hours.

Heat the stock to the boiling point. Remove from the heat and sprinkle the gelatine over it. Stir until dissolved. Leave to cool to room temperature. Stir in the basil and pour this aspic into a rectangular dish about 30 × 15 cm/12 × 16 inches. Leave to set in the refrigerator for about 2 hours.

In a bowl, whisk the Parmesan into the mayonnaise. Divide the mixture between six small individual moulds or custard cups. Drain the eggs well and place one in each mould on top of the mayonnaise.

Dice the basil aspic and sprinkle over the egg. Dust with paprika and serve. The moulds may be completed well in advance and only the paprika added at the last minute.

Riches of the Soil
by
Fynes MORYSON

ALL THE FIELDS ARE FULL OF FIGTREES, NOT SMALL AS with us, but as big in the body as some Appel-trees, and they have broad leaves. The fruite hath the forme of a long peare, and a blacke skinne, and a red juyce, being to be sucked like sugar in taste. Neither doe I thinke any fruite to bee more pleasant then this pulled from the tree, I say pulled from the tree, because the drie figges exported, are not in taste comparable thereunto. In the fields of upper Italy are great plenty of Almond trees, so as you would say, that a whole Province is but one Garden. Like plenty have they of Olive trees, which yeeld a sweet oyle, used by them in stead of butter, and in forraigne parts for wholsomnesse, yet I cannot think that it can be wholsome when it is heated, as the Italians use it to fry meates. They have some, but not so great plenty of Pomegranates, which tree is not unlike that of the white Rose, but the leaves are little, and the flowers and the buds of a red colour. The Husbandmen make ditches about the rootes of all these fruite trees, and the inhabitants of pleasant Italy are notable in all kind of Husbandrie. The Cypresse, Pople, and Oake trees, grow in many places, but are little esteemed, as bearing no fruite.

Italy upon the Hilles and Mountaines lying towards the Sunne, yeelds rich Wines, and very nourishing, yet some out of experience say, they are not wholsome for fat men, as causing obstructions, and hindring the passage of the urine, and other evacuations: but I am sure they are more pleasant in taste, then any other wine whatsoever brought into England that ever I tasted.

AN ITINERARY, FYNES MORYSON, 1605–17.

A Dish with an Open Pomegranate, a Grasshopper, a Snail and Two Chestnuts

35

Risotto agli Scampi

"THEN WE [*in Italy*] HAVE RICE, which is eaten in many countries, but grown in few. We plant it in low-lying places, under water. It has a good yield, and is a most useful crop. It is a good food for the able-bodied, but hard to digest."

90 g/3 oz/6 tbsp unsalted butter
450 g/1 lb uncooked scampi or shrimp tails, peeled
salt and pepper
1.2 litres/2 pints/5 cups fish stock
2 tbsp chopped onion
480 g/17 oz/2 cups Arborio rice
120 ml/4 fl oz whipping cream

IN A LARGE WIDE PAN, MELT 15 G/½ OZ/1 TBSP BUTTER. Add the scampi or shrimp and sauté over medium heat for 2 minutes. Season to taste with salt and pepper. Set aside. Heat the stock to boiling point.

In a medium saucepan, melt the rest of the butter over low heat. Add the onion and cook until translucent, about 5 minutes. Increase the heat to medium, add the rice and stir until well heated, about 2 minutes. Add 3 ladles of fish stock and continue to cook, stirring constantly.

Gradually add the rest of the stock, so that the rice is always covered with a veil of liquid.

After 12 minutes add the scampi or shrimp and cream.

Exactly 14 minutes after adding the first ladles of stock, remove the saucepan from the heat. Season with salt and pepper. Cover the saucepan and leave it to stand for 2 minutes. Transfer the risotto to a warm platter and serve immediately.

I sometimes use sliced lobster, crabmeat or scallops instead of scampi in this risotto. If you would like to add colour, sprinkle the risotto with chopped parsley just before serving it. While the risotto itself should have a creamy texture, the rice grains should be firm to the bite.

The Mercato Vecchio
by
Giuseppe CONTI

ONCE YOU ENTERED CALIMARA DE BACCANO OPPOSITE the Loggias of the Mercato Nuovo, you could say you were already in the Old Market. On the corner at the left there was the famous store of the tobacconist Valenti – renowned for its vinegars, barley water and muskmelon preserved in alcohol. Here the street narrowed immediately, full of a busy crowd of servants, cooks with the shopping baskets of those days, and people who had neither servants nor cooks and did their own shopping, skimping their *quattrini* and trying to spend them *"co'gomiti"* (with the elbow) as the Florentines used to say.

In this stretch, up to Via della Sette Botteghe, there were linoleum makers, hemp-sellers and ironmongers; alongside the Passo dell'Arte della Lana there were the fryers of black sausage, gnocchi, rice-cakes, and something of everything. In the evenings, especially on Friday and Saturday, and on Lenten vigils, the scene in this part of Calimara was truly fascinating.

Flickering oil lamps or torches on the end of a pole, with the flames of the burners on which the frying-pans sizzled away, giving off sharp smells of fish and dried cod gave off flashes of reddish light in the distance, with very curious play of light and shade.

The fryers shouted to attract the public, and the public hurried to gobble up the meal consisting of apple and artichoke fritters, salted cod, fish from the Arno and courgette flowers, according to the season. In this area, the bustle between midnight and one o'clock was enormous.

FIRENZE VECCHIA, GIUSEPPE CONTI, 1899.

Mischief at Court
by
Janet ROSS

IN HONOUR OF THE VISIT OF THE PRINCESS ANNA de'Medici with her husband, the Archduke Ferdinand of Austria and his two brothers, and of the Duke of Mantua and his wife, who was a Medici, splendid festivals were given in the Palazzo Pitti, while a ballet on horseback, led by Cosimo, the youthful heir to the throne, was performed in the amphitheatre in the Boboli gardens by fifty-two cavaliers magnificently dressed and mounted on well-broken horses. Vincenzio Martinelli gives a curious description of the tomboy games of Marguerite Louise. "Cosimo had obliged the Grand Duchess to send back to France all the gentlemen and ladies of her court, and only one Frenchman, a cook, remained. The Grand Duke gave himself up to devotion and solitude and governed his family, as he did his state, like Tiberius, and allowed his wife no amusement save a small concert for two or three hours every evening. The Grand Duchess, who was very young, found these concerts monotonous, or perhaps, being born in France, did not care for Italian music, so as a diversion she used to send for her French cook, who came with his long apron and white cap,

just as he was dressed for cooking the dinner. Now this cook either dreaded, or pretended to dread, being tickled, and the princess, aware of his weakness, took great pleasure in tickling him, while he made all those contortions, screams and cries proper to people who cannot bear to be tickled. Thus the princess tickled the cook, and he defended himself, shouting and running from one side of the room to the other, which made her laugh immoderately. When tired of such romps she would take a pillow from her bed and belabour the cook on the face and on the body, whilst he, shouting aloud, hid himself now under, now on, the very bed of the princess, where she continued to beat him, until tired out with laughing and beating she sank exhausted into a chair. This noble amusement continued for some time before the Grand Duke knew of it; but one evening it happened that the cook was very drunk, and therefore shouted louder than usual, and the Grand Duke, whose apartments were five or six rooms distant from those of the Grand Duchess, heard the noise and went to discover the cause. As he entered the room the Grand Duchess was just beating her cook with a pillow on the grand-

THE PITTI PALACE

ducal bed, and the Prince, horrified at so novel a sight, instantly condemned the cook to the galleys (but I believe he was eventually pardoned), and scolding the lady with the utmost severity, with a bearing more princely than marital, he forbad her ever again to indulge in such conduct. The princess resented being thus taken to task, and was exceedingly angry. After passing the whole night in fury and in tears she determined to return to France, and sent one of her gentlemen to the Grand Duke to inform him of her resolution. He coldly replied that the Grand Duchess had better reflect on the consequences of such a step, which he would in no way oppose. It ended by the Grand Duchess returning to France, leaving two sons and a daughter, who were the last of the great house of Medici.

FLORENTINE PALACES AND THEIR STORIES, JANET ROSS, 1905.

A Dish of Plums, with Jasmine and Walnuts

40

Tagliatelle alle Noci

NOODLES WITH A NUT CREAM

"WE HAVE WALNUTS, which are common everywhere. The green ones start to be good about the feast of St Lawrence [10 August], and are highly esteemed and eaten by the gentry, who consider the dried ones to be rather coarse and unrefined."

450 g/1 lb dry egg noodles
120 ml/4 fl oz whipping cream
60 g/3 oz/6 tbsp unsalted butter
90 g/3 oz shelled walnuts, chopped
60 g/3 oz/¾ cup freshly grated Parmesan cheese
salt and pepper

BRING 5 LITRES/8 PINTS/5 QUARTS OF SALTED WATER TO the boil in a large pot. Drop in the noodles and cook until *al dente*.

Meanwhile, heat the cream and butter in a saucepan until melted and smooth. Add the walnuts and remove from the heat. Drain the noodles, mix with the walnut cream, and sprinkle with the Parmesan. Season to taste and serve very hot.

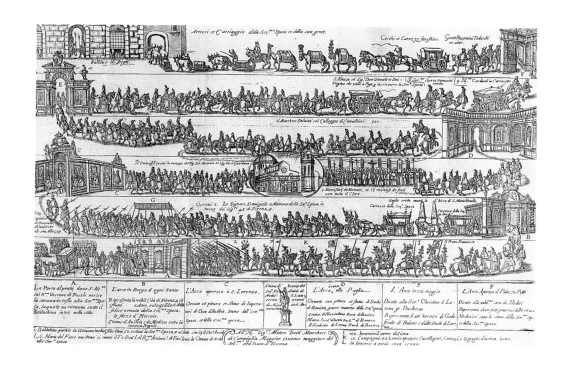

MARIA MADDALENA'S ENTRANCE INTO FLORENCE, 1608

A Banquet at the Palazzo Vecchio
by
Janet ROSS

THE MARRIAGE OF COSIMO DE' MEDICI, SON OF THE Grand Duke Ferdinando I, with the Archduchess Maria Maddalena of Austria, was celebrated with extraordinary pomp in 1608. A great banquet was given in the Hall of the Five Hundred to the Florentine nobility, of which an anonymous eyewitness has left a long description. Two hundred and forty ladies sat opposite the Princes, as "being more fair to look upon than men," and after dinner appeared a Venus' shell gliding forward on sham waves, which bore Zephyr, the messenger of the goddess who, stopping in front of the bride, offered her all his mistress could give. Then came the chariot of Venus drawn by black sparrows in which sat Love, who declared all he had was hers. On the raising of a curtain at the end of the hall, angels floating among clouds were seen, who chanted:

"*E sol risuona,*
E Maddalena intuona
La valle, il colle, il monte, il prato il bosco
Di questo lido Tosco,
E'l Ciel, l'Aria, e la Terra e l'Onda piena
Cosmo, Cosmo risponde, e Maddalena."

After this the Princes retired by the corridor to the Palazzo Pitti, "the Archduchess graciously inviting the ladies present to follow her as far as the gallery, where a long row of tables were laden with delicate sugarplums and confectionery. What they could not eat or carry away was seized by the populace which streamed in; the Princes watched with great amusement the demolition of all that rare food, and then withdrew to their rooms."

FLORENTINE PALACES AND THEIR STORIES, JANET ROSS, 1905.

Faraona alle Pesche

Roast Guinea Fowl with Peaches

"This delicate fruit is usually eaten raw. Some eat peaches unpeeled,
after wiping the skin with a clean cloth, and quote in justification the
saying:
A l'amico monda il fico, e il persico al nemico.
Peel a fig for a friend, and a peach for an enemy."

6 loose-stone peaches
2 tbsp lemon juice
pinch of grated nutmeg
1 guinea fowl or hen, about 1.8 kg/3 ½ lb
1 tbsp chopped fresh rosemary
1 tbsp chopped fresh sage
salt and pepper
90 g/3 oz pancetta, sliced very thin
15 g/½ oz/1 tbsp unsalted butter
2 tbsp extra virgin olive oil
120 ml/4 fl oz dry white wine
2 tbsp brandy

BLANCH THE PEACHES BRIEFLY IN BOILING WATER TO loosen the skins, then drain. Peel, cut in half and remove the stones. Sprinkle the hollows with lemon juice and nutmeg. Arrange the peach halves, cut sides up, on a baking sheet. Bake in a preheated 180°C/350°F/gas 4 oven for about 20 minutes. Remove and set aside.

Wash, dry and truss the guinea fowl. Sprinkle it with the herbs mixed with a little salt and pepper. Wrap it in the thin slices of pancetta. Set in a roasting pan with butter and oil.

Bake in the preheated oven for about 1 ½ hours.

Remove from the oven and transfer the guinea fowl to a warm serving platter. Keep warm.

Skim off the fat from the cooking juices and put the roasting pan over low heat. Add the white wine and scrape the pan with a wooden spoon to deglaze the sediments. Add the brandy and boil to evaporate the alcohol. Add the peaches to the pan and heat through. Arrange the peaches around the guinea fowl and pour the deglazed cooking juices over it.

A Bowl with Peaches and Plums

45

THE BAPTISTERY AND PROCESSION OF CORPUS DOMINI

A Monastic Repast in the Appenines
by
Lady Anne MILLER

LETTER FROM FLORENCE DATED DECEMBER 18TH, 1770.

THE MONKS THEMSELVES TAKE BY TURN THE INSPECtion of the kitchen. You know the church in all countries inclines to good fare, and this is not a rigid order. Two of the Monks did not appear; I suppose one was employed in the kitchen, and the other, perhaps, indisposed. The superior made us many excuses for the bad fare we should have, and for our being obliged to wait for supper; saying, they themselves had already supped, that they had scarce any provisions in the house, and being a *maigre* day also (for it was Saturday) he hoped we would excuse etc. However, we did not wait a quarter of an hour for supper. They lamented much the not having previous notice of our arrival, as they would have given us a better reception, and added many polite things; but before they had finished, the two servants appeared with a small table for M--- and me and laid a cloth and a lay-over upon it, in our English fashion, of the finest damask I have ever seen; it was callendered and pinched, forming a Mosaic pattern; the napkins were curiously folded, the plates of the finest old China; spoons, knives, forks &c saltsellers of silver of the most elegant fashion, and so clean, that they appeared quite new; they served one dish at a time; first, an admirable gravy-soup in a beautiful tureen of the same China as the plates; they removed this with a *poularde a la braise* as good as you ever saw from Bresse; then a fry *très recherchée*, after the Italian ecclesiastical fashion; then a pigeon *pattue don le cul étoit farci* garnished with small cakes, made of a kind of paste, quite agreeable to eat with the pigeon. The dessert consisted of grapes so well conserved that they seemed as just gathered, Burey pears, fine chestnuts roasted, and excellent Parmesan cheese. They were quite teasing whilst we supped, with their apologies for such miserable fare as they termed it. During our repast three crystal carraffes were set on the table, which held about a pint each; one filled with an excellent red wine, another with white, and a third with water. At the dessert a bottle of wine was produced, and the Superior pressed us to try it. M--- said it was the finest Cypress he had ever tasted. Was not this an elegant supper for a quarter of an hour's preparation?

LADY ANNE MILLER "LETTERS FROM ITALY"

Spuma di Prosciutto e Fichi

PROSCIUTTO MOUSSE IN FIG SAUCE

"I MUST NOT FORGET TO MENTION FIGS, which we have in vast quantities, and which everyone eats raw. We do not have many dried figs in my part of Italy, though they are common in other regions, and are very good indeed, particularly with almonds. Confectioners preserve them whole with peeled almonds in the shape of Dutch cheeses, a delicious sweetmeat, which they keep to eat during Lent."

450 g/1 lb thinly sliced prosciutto
450 ml/15 fl oz whipping cream
1 tbsp powdered unflavoured gelatine
12 fresh, ripe figs

PUT THE PROSCIUTTO IN A FOOD PROCESSOR FITTED with metal blades. Blend until smooth and homogenous. Heat half the cream over low heat, then remove from the heat and sprinkle over the gelatine. Stir until dissolved, and add to the ham. Whip the rest of the cream until stiff and fold into the ham and cream mixture.

Wet a 17.5 cm/7 inch mould with cold water and fill with the ham mousse. Chill for about 5 hours (it can be left in the refrigerator for up to 12 hours). Peel the figs, put in a food processor fitted with metal blades. Blend to a smooth cream.

To remove the mousse from the mould, dip the base of the container in a saucepan full of boiling water for 5 seconds, set an upturned plate on top and turn over, holding them tightly together. Pour the fig sauce around the mousse and serve.

A Dish of Figs, with Jasmine and Small Pears

TALL FRUIT BOWL WITH PEACHES, BENEATH, CRAB APPLES AND FIGS

A Marriage between the Rucellai and Medici
by
Guido BIAGI

GILDED BY THE FLAMING SUN OF JUNE, GREEN FES-toons swung proudly across the street which was the scene of the wedding, festoons that brought into high relief the shields which ornamented the house-fronts, and which were quartered half with the arms of the Medici and half with those of the Rucellai. Opposite the palace, in the little piazza in front of the *loggia*, had been erected a triangular platform. Below, on wooden planks, were laid tapestries, and precious tapestries also covered the benches placed around. The ends of the great blue *velarium* hung down here and there to the ground like aerial columns. On one side of that great tent there was a large sideboard, on which glittered silver vessels and dishes wrought by the best gold and silver smiths in Florence. The richness of these adornments presaged the magnificence of the banquet that was preparing. The kitchen had been placed in the street by the side of the palace, where, counting cooks and underlings, fifty persons were at work. The noise was great; Via della Vigna was crowded with people from one end to the other. The men who had decked the façade were succeeded by the servants who carried the presents from friends, clients, and relations; peasants, gardeners, and shop-people brought vic-tuals; pipers and trumpeters were preparing their music, and the cavaliers were making ready for the tilting-match. That Sunday, June 8, 1466, soon after dawn, the crowd began to arrive from all sides at the palace where the wedding was to take place. There also came, welcome and promising sight to the curious, quartered bullocks, casks of Greek wine, and as many capons as could hang on a staff, borne on the shoulders of two stout peasants; bars of buffalo-cheese, turkeys in pairs, barrels of ordinary wine and choice sweet wine, baskets full of pomegranates, hampers of large sea-fish, crates of little silver-scaled fish from the Arno, birds, hares, cream-cheeses packed in fresh green rushes, baskets full of sweetmeats, tarts, and other delicate confectionery, prepared by the fair hands of some gentle nun.

MEN AND MANNERS OF OLD FLORENCE, GUIDO BIAGI, 1909.

Palombe alla Ghiotta

WILD PIGEONS STEWED IN RED WINE

"AUTUMN IN ITALY is so temperate and delightful, with such an abundance of every kind of fruit, that we have the saying:
L'autunno per la bocca et la primavera per l'occhio.
Spring is for looking, autumn for tasting."

3 wild pigeons or squab
1 litre/1 ¾ pints/1 quart red wine
100 ml/3 ½ fl oz vinegar
4 garlic cloves
1 sprig of fresh rosemary
1 small bunch of fresh sage, tied together
1 small onion, quartered
100 g/3 ½ oz prosciutto
4 tbsp extra virgin olive oil
4 anchovy fillets in oil
1 tbsp capers in vinegar, rinsed
1 lemon wedge
1 thin slice of bread
salt and pepper

CLEAN THE PIGEONS, LEAVING HEADS AND FEET ON, if still attached. Place in a flameproof casserole with all the other ingredients and cook over low heat for about 1 ½ hours. Take the pigeons from the casserole and remove and discard heads and feet, if necessary. Halve the pigeons lengthwise and reserve. Continue to heat the sauce for about another hour until it thickens. Remove the rosemary and sage and purée the sauce in a food mill or food processor. Return the pigeon halves to the casserole with the sauce, reheat for 10 minutes and serve.

THE OLD MAN OF ARTIMINO

53

Salsa di Pere

PEAR SAUCE

"EARLY IN AUGUST we enjoy *gnocchi* or *sozzobuoni* pears. They are about the same size as the ones you call Catherine pears, and I have never seen them, let alone eaten them, outside Italy. They fill the mouth with an unbelievably delicious juice, which tastes rather like melons."

450 g/1 lb pears
30 g/1 oz/2 tbsp unsalted butter
1 cinnamon stick, about 2.5 cm/1 inch long
1 clove
2 tbsp sugar
1 tsp powdered mustard

PEEL AND CORE THE PEARS AND SLICE VERY THINLY. In a saucepan, combine the butter, sliced pears, cinnamon stick, clove, sugar and mustard. Cover the saucepan and cook over very low heat until the pears are very soft, about 20 minutes.

Push the mixture through a sieve. Reheat the sauce before serving.

I usually serve this sauce with the pigeons on page 52, but obviously it is suitable for all roast game. Without the mustard, it can also be served with cooked fruit, lemon sorbet or apple pie. It may be kept in the fridge for about 12 hours and reheated just before serving.

Of the Grape they Feed
by
Sir Robert DALLINGTON

A SURVEY OF THE GREAT DUKES STATE OF TUSCANIE, IN THE YEARE OF OUR LORD 1596

THE VINE WHICH WITHOUT COMPARISON IS THE greatest commoditie of *Tuscany*, if not of *Italy*, hath these uses. Of the Grape they feed, of the juyce they make Wine; of the shreddings they make small bundles, like our Fagots of gaule in *Cambridge*, & sell them for two *quatrini* a peece for firing: of their leaves feed their Oxen, or else dung their land; & lastly of the stones they feed their Pigions, which after the Vintage they riddle out of the Grape being dryed, and these they sell at 20 *soldi* the *Staio*.

There are divers sorts of Grapes, the names of such as I remember are these; *Uva Canaiola*, good either to eate or for Wine; *Passerina* a small Grape, whereof Sparrowes feed, good onely for Wine; *Trebbiana* the best sort of white Grapes for Wine, whereof they make their *Vin Trebbiano, Zibibbo*; these are dryed for Lent: *Moscatello* with a taste like Muske,

not for wine, but to eate: *Uva grossa* not to eate, but for Wine; *Raverutta*, of it selfe neither to eate, nor for Wine, but a few of these put among a great vessell of Wine, giveth it a colour, for which use it onely serveth: *San Columbana* and *Rimaldesca* a very delicate Grape, either for Wine or to eate; *Lugliola* which hath his name of the moneth of Iuly wherein it is ripe, better to eate than for Wine; and lastly *Cerisiana*, named for the taste it hath like a Cherry better for Wine than to eate.

They have also as many names for their Figs, the best are the *Brugiotti*, which being needlesse to recount, as also to stand thus particularly upon all the rest, I will omit to speake: only in a word I will speake of the Mulberry, which being another of the greatest commodities of *Tuscany* I may not forget.

SIR ROBERT DALLINGTON, 1605.

Cherries like Plums . . .
by
Hester PIOZZI

OBSERVATIONS ON A JOURNEY THROUGH ITALY

THE FRUITS IN THIS PLACE BEGIN TO ASTONISH ME; such cherries did I never yet see, or even hear tell of, as when I caught the laquais de place weighing two of them in a scale to see if they came to an ounce. These are, in the London street phrase, cherries like plums, in size at least, but in flavour they far exceed them, being exactly of the kind that we call bleeding-hearts, hard to the bite and parting easily from the stone, which is proportionately small. Figs, too, are here in such perfection, that it is not easy for an English gardener to guess at their excellence; for it is not by superior size, but taste and colour, that they are distinguished – small and green on the outside, a bright full crimson within – and we eat them with raw ham, and truly delicious is the dainty. By raw ham, I mean ham cured, not boiled or roasted. It is no wonder, though, that fruits should mature in such a sun as this is, which, to give a just notion of its penetrating fire, I will take leave to tell my country-women is so violent, that I use no other method of heating the pinching-irons to curl my hair than that of poking them out at a south window, with the handles shut in, and the glasses darkened to keep us from being actually fired in his beams. Before I leave off speaking about the fruit, I must add that both fig and cherry are produced by standards, that the stawberries here are small and high-flavoured, like our 'woods', and that there are no other. England affords greater variety in that kind of fruit than any nation; and as to peaches, nectarines, or greengage plums, I have seen none yet. Lady Cowper has made us a present of a small pineapple, but the Italians have no taste to it. Here is sun enough to ripen them without hot-houses, I am sure, though they repeatedly told us at Milan and Venice that this was the coolest place to pass the summer in, because of the Apennine mountains.

HESTER PIOZZI, 1789.

A Dish of Cherries, with Figs and Medlars

Polpette in Salsa di Mele

MEATBALLS IN APPLE SAUCE

"ONE OF THESE [*Italian apples*] WE CALL THE PARADISE APPLE; it is about the same size as the one you have here called the 'two-year apple', but its skin is yellow and speckled with little blood-red spots. The longer it is kept, the better it becomes. These apples not only taste delicious, but have a wonderful sweet smell, and will scent linen sheets if laid between them. The peel, thrown on a shovel of coals, will fill a room with the aroma. It is also used to perfume ointments."

4 slices of crustless white coarse-textured bread
5–6 tbsp milk
600 g/1 ¼ lb minced (ground) beef
2 size 5/medium eggs
2 tbsp finely grated Parmesan cheese
120 g/4 oz mortadella, finely chopped
1 tbsp juniper berries, crushed
salt
2 cooking apples
60 g/2 oz/4 tbsp butter
1 tsp freshly grated horseradish

SOAK THE BREAD IN THE MILK FOR ABOUT 30 MINUTES. Drain and squeeze out excess milk.

In a bowl combine the beef, eggs, Parmesan, mortadella, bread and juniper berries. Season with a little salt. Mix until well amalgamated.

Using your hands, roll the mixture into 12 balls and flatten with the palms of your hands.

Peel, core and slice the apples. In a frying pan, heat half the butter. Add the sliced apples, 4 tbsp water and a pinch of salt. Cover and cook over low heat for about 6 minutes. Pour the cooked apples and their juices into a blender and add the grated horseradish. Blend well and set aside.

In the frying pan heat the rest of the butter. Add the meatballs and cook for 2 minutes on each side. Add the apple sauce to the pan. Stir, then cover and cook for 2 minutes. Serve hot.

A Dish with Apples and Almonds

59

THE FESTA DEGLI OMAGGI

La Festa di San Giovanni
by
Giuseppe CONTI

UNDER THE MEDICI PRINCIPATE, THE FEASTS OF ST John Baptist lost their austerely grandiose character; the city, instead of having the air of a rich and happy state, took on that of gilded servitude, and the feasts had more of the exoticism and apparatus of a theatrical spectacle than the magnificent expression of a free people.

On the days of Saint John Baptist, in the former Piazza de'Signori, white wine was sold by the *soma* (old measure of capacity = app 150 litres), and meatballs in fine dishes exposed on many tables; fresh chickpeas were sold in bunches for the amusement of the plebs, and those were called *spassatempo*, and likewise certain very sweet cakes, made of flour, honey and pepper, which if we trace their verbal origin, were called '*confortini*' because they were meant to comfort the stomach. Here many broom-heads were burned on this evening, where the most select gentry amused themselves with all sorts of roguery, and on the tower of Palazzo Vecchio, fireworks.

There were crackers, catherine wheels and rockets. In the spacious hall of that palace, known as the Salone del Cinquecento, on the following day spirited dances were held by the young people of both sexes from the neighbouring villages. Perhaps because of the over-frequent couplings which took place on these occasions or because of too much cooperation in the multiplication of the human race, these were later "completely forbidden".

Fagiuoli has also described the *palio*, and concludes: "Thus on that day there was much exultation and feasting and that blessed banner fluttered at the high point of the campanile, which caused certain bats to come forth who cannot see by day; and there was, in short, much rejoicing and merriment."

FIRENZE VECCHIA, GIUSEPPE CONTI, 1899.

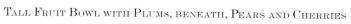

TALL FRUIT BOWL WITH PLUMS, BENEATH, PEARS AND CHERRIES

Coniglio alle Prugne

RABBIT WITH PRUNES

"PLUMS START TO BE GOOD about this time [*autumn*], but since they are known everywhere I don't need to say much about them, except that they are healthy to eat and better fresh than dried. They should only be eaten when fully ripe and during meals; not afterwards as you do in this country."

12 large, plump prunes
1 rabbit, about 1.8 kg/3 ½ lb
3 tbsp extra virgin olive oil
1 tbsp flour
240 ml/8 fl oz dry white wine
salt and pepper

PUT THE PRUNES IN A BOWL, COVER WITH WATER AND leave to soak for 30 minutes. Drain.

Cut the rabbit into bite-size pieces. Heat the oil in a wide shallow pan, add the rabbit pieces and cook over moderate heat until golden brown on all sides. Sprinkle with the flour. Add the prunes, pour in the wine and add salt and pepper to taste. Cover and cook over low heat for about 1 ½ hours, adding water when necessary to keep the cooking juices moist.

Transfer the rabbit and prunes to a serving dish and serve very hot.

A Grand Chariot Race
by
Giuseppe CONTI

THE GRAND DUKE AND THE WHOLE COURT AND followers, in a gala procession, preceded by two out-riders and escorted by eight noble guards and two riding-masters called "di sportello", arrived a little before the race, and since this was virtually a horseriding spectacle, the Duke was dressed as a colonel of the Austrian Cavalry, with the white uniform with gold braiding at the collar and cuffs; knee-breeches and riding boots, and the helmet with the gilded crest, and a great deal of fancy decoration with the two-headed eagle on the crown. He thought he made a fine impression but this wretched helmet, held backwards, ruined the effect. He would have been better dressed as a friar!

The people who waited on the Sovereign, with a special ticket from the Master of the Royal Household, went to enjoy the palio in the Court Box, leaving a free space in their own seats for the pages and their tutors. The ladies in waiting and the non-noble persons, also armed with the same tickets, went to the terrace of the forage warehouse, and to the three windows of the Casa Puliti. The others, domestics and servants, went to the stalls reserved for the common people.

However, the greatest honour, after this, was bestowed upon Architect Baccani, since the Grand Duke each year advised him that he would send the little Archdukes to his house, one of the most beautiful in the piazza.

Before the race, on the Sovereign's terrace, "abundant refreshments were served", then the signal was given for the race to begin. The expectation was very high, as the effect of the amphitheatre was stupendous: those thousands of people seated in the stalls, the crowd lined up behind the hemp curtain, the windows of the houses and the terraces crowded, some people on the roofs, who even risked climbing right to the top to see the race, with the danger that they would fall and end up in the piazza and smash a collar bone or worse; the whole thing was an imposing spectacle.

After so many false moves, premature starts by one or other of the chariots, or failure to start by another, the race finally began. One could hear a pin drop. The charioteers were dressed in Roman costume to keep in character with the chariots; one white, one red, one yellow and one green. As soon as those four carts launched themselves at full pelt

THE CHARIOT RACE

around the circle, of which they had to make three rounds, the race began – at least in appearance – to be sharply contested. In fact all four charioteers had already agreed on the outcome, and the so-called sport was a magnificent sham. At certain moments when the chariots formed a tight group, it looked as if everything might end in disaster. And then, lo and behold, from the moving cloud of dust in which they were enveloped like a halo, the victorious chariot would emerge. Then there was an outburst of applause, a confusion of shouts, 'evviva's', to welcome the victor, who feigned great emotion, considering that he had known since the morning.

After the palio of the chariots, the amphitheatre and the piazza emptied, and all the crowd headed off to the Lungarno to watch the famous and longed-for firework display.

FIRENZE VECCHIA, GIUSEPPE CONTI, 1899.

65

Salsa di Ciliege

CHERRY SAUCE

"CORNELIAN CHERRIES ARE GOOD NOW [*autumn*]. They are a little red fruit, longish in shape and as big as a medium-sized olive. They have very hard stones, a bitter flavour and are even more astringent than sorb-apples. This is not what I call a serious fruit; it is more for little children and pregnant women than grown men."

450 g/1 lb ripe dark cherries
1 clove
180 g/6 oz/scant 1 cup sugar
grated zest of ½ orange
240 ml/8 fl oz red wine
1 tbsp potato flour or arrowroot

STONE (PIT) THE CHERRIES AND SET ASIDE ABOUT 15 stones. Crush the stones and tie them in muslin or cheesecloth with the clove.

In a saucepan combine the cherries, sugar, orange zest, red wine and the bag of cherry stones. Bring to the boil, then lower the heat and simmer until the cooking juices become syrupy and will coat a spoon, about 15 minutes. Discard the bag of stones and transfer the cherries and syrup to a blender.

Add the potato flour or arrowroot and purée until creamy.

Return the sauce to the saucepan and heat gently for a couple of minutes, without boiling, before serving.

The crushed cherry stones add a wonderful perfume to this sauce. Although it is generally served with game birds or with meat this sauce is also excellent with a sweet, particularly on chocolate ice cream. You can also serve the sauce cold, in which case just omit the potato flour.

A Dish of Cherries with a Bean and a Hornet

Of the Wines of Italy
by
Fynes MORYSON

THE ITALIANS HOLD IT A GREAT SHAME TO BE DRUNKEN, they sometimes salute one another with a cup, in manner of a health, but leave it to his pleasure when he will pledge them, and then he salutes him that drunke to him, as well as him to whom he drinkes, saying; *Faccio ragione a vos' signoria, brindisi a vos Signoria.* Sir I pledge you, and I drink to you Sir. The word Brindisi comes of the Dutch phrase, *Ich brings euch,* I will bring it to you, used when they drinke to any man, and this shewes the custome is borrowed from the Germans, and used by the obsequious Italians to please them, yet abhorring from drunkennesse, so pleasing to the Germans.

Italy yeeldes excellent Wines, and the common red wine is held very nourishing, so as the fairest Women will dine with the same, and a sop of bread dipped in it, thinking it will make them fat, (which kind of Women the Venetians most love, all things else being equall), yea, and more faire: So as they Proverbially say; *Chi beve bianco, piscia bianco, a chi beve rosso, avanza il colore.* He that drinkes white, pisses white, he that drinkes red, gaines the colour: These are the most famous Wines of Italy. La lagrima di Christo, (the teare of Christ) and like wines neere Cinqueterre in Liguria: La vernaza, and the white Muskadine, especially that of Monte-fiaschoni in Toscany: Cecubum and Falernum in the King-dome of Naples, and Prosecho in Histria. In generall the grapes that grow high upon Elme-trees in the plaine, as in Lombardy, & especially the grapes of Modena, yeeld very small Wines, but those that grow upon hils and mountaines, resting on short stakes, yeeld very rich Wines. In the shops where they sell Muskadines, there be continually boyes attending with little wigges of sweete bread and Junkets, which the Italians dip in the wine; and having thus broke their fasts in winter time, they commonly eate no more till supper.

AN ITINERARY, FYNES MORYSON, 1605–17.

68

Arista di Maiale al Finocchio

ROAST PORK WITH FENNEL

"WE PRESERVE QUANTITIES OF FRESH FENNEL in good white wine vinegar and eat it in summer and in winter when offering drinks to friends between meals. We also serve this pickle with fruit on special occasions, when fresh fennel is not to be had.
Fennel seeds are gathered in the autumn. We flavour various dishes with them, and eat them on their own after meals."

1 sprig of fresh rosemary
4 garlic cloves
salt and pepper
2 ½ tsp fennel seeds
1 pork loin, about 1.2 kg/ 2 ½ lb, bones split
60 g/2 oz/4 tbsp butter
1 tbsp extra virgin olive oil
1 fennel bulb
120 ml/4 fl oz milk
240 ml/8 fl oz white wine

FINELY CHOP THE ROSEMARY AND GARLIC. ADD SALT, pepper and the fennel seeds. Stuff this mixture into the cuts in the pork where the bones were split. Place the meat in a roasting pan with half of the butter and the olive oil and roast in a preheated 170°C/325°F/gas 3 oven for about 2 hours.

Roughly chop the fennel, then cook in a covered pan with the remaining butter and a little water over low heat until tender. Transfer to a blender, add the milk and blend until smooth.

When the meat is cooked, slice and arrange on a serving platter. Keep warm. Pour off the fat from the roasting pan, and deglaze with the white wine. Boil for a couple of minutes, then add the fennel mixture, mix well and strain over the meat.

Additional fennel sauce can be served at the table.

Fave in Salsa al Limone

Broad Beans in Lemon Sauce

"Fresh broad beans come next. We eat them at the end of a meal with a
salty cheese from Crete or Sardinia, or failing that with Parmesan, and
always with pepper. If there is no cheese, we just eat them with salt."

600 g/1 ¼ lb shelled young broad (fava) beans
30 g/1 oz/2 tbsp unsalted butter
2 tbsp flour
240 ml/8 fl oz light chicken stock
salt and pepper
juice of 1 lemon
2 egg yolks

Bring a saucepan of salted water to the boil. Add the broad beans and cook until just tender, about 5 minutes.

Meanwhile, in another saucepan melt half the butter over moderate heat. Add the flour and stir well. Stirring constantly, gradually add the stock and allow to boil for a few minutes. Remove from the heat and season to taste with salt and pepper. Stir in the rest of the butter, the lemon juice and egg yolks.

Drain the beans and arrange on a warm platter. Coat with the sauce and serve at once.

This lemon sauce is also very good with other vegetables, particularly asparagus, fennel and artichokes. But obviously the cooking times for the vegetables vary.

A DISH OF BROAD BEANS

71

A Guild Dinner
by
Giuseppe CONTI

THERE WERE TWENTY-FOUR ASSOCIATES IN ALL — twelve who were from the greater Guilds (Arti) and twelve from the lesser ones.

The first dinner of this Association of the *Cazzuola* (the Trowel) was held in the summer of 1512, and was arranged by Giuliano Bugiardini, who was the *"Signore"* of the company for that evening. He had given the order that everyone should come dressed in the clothes that they liked best; and in fact at the appointed hour they appeared in "the most beautiful and bizarre extravaganzas of dress that it is possible to imagine". They were placed at table "in accordance with the quality of their dress", so that those wearing princely habits took the most decorous places, those dressed in rich or gentlemanly fashion were placed next to them, while those who were in the habits of the poorer people sat in "the lowest and most humble ranks".

At the dinner for the Feast of St Andrew, arranged by the Rustici and Bugiardini, they all came dressed in workmens' and builders' clothes, complete with trowels and hammers. In the first room, the *Signore* showed them the plan of a building due to be constructed. As he placed the master masons at the table, the workmen began bringing in trays of lasagne and ricotta with sugar, to lay the foundations.

The mortar was made up of cheese and spices to flavour the lasagne, and for the gravel chips they used large segments of *berlingozzi* (a crisp ring cake shaped like a doughnut). The building-blocks, tiles and flat surfaces were carried in in big baskets by the workmen and loaves in the form of bas-reliefs were brought in on litters. When the foundations had been laid in this way, and when it seemed to the masons that the whole work had been done according to the strict rules of the art, it was then decided that it should be smashed to pieces. All twenty-four companions, armed with their trowels, then began gleefully demolishing the foundations, in which they found cakes, little pieces of pigs' liver, and other such things.

No sooner had this masterpiece been destroyed than a tall column swathed in cooked veal tripe was brought in. This too was deemed unsatisfactory by the architects, so the wrapping was removed and the companions began eating once more,

SERVICE AT A BANQUET

tucking in to the boiled meat and capons which were inside. These were eaten with the same gusto as the base of the column, made out of Parmesan, and the capitol, which had been ingeniously formed out of inlays of roast capon, veal liver and a moulding of tongues. After the column, a section of lintel, frieze and cornice was brought in, composed of so many delicious foods that it was a miracle that everyone present did not explode. So, when they had filled their bodies, the noise and the songs began, and a play was performed. This was how the *Cazzuola* held its meetings every year.

FATTI E ANEDOTTI DI STORIA FIORENTINA C13TH–18TH, GIUSEPPE CONTI, 1902.

Carciofi con Piselli in Umido

BRAISED ARTICHOKES AND PEAS

"IF YOU DO NOT FEEL LIKE EATING ARTICHOKES raw, select some small ones and cut off the tips of the pointed outer leaves. Boil them first in fresh water to take away the bitterness, and then finish cooking them in rich beef or chicken broth. Serve them in a shallow dish on slices of bread moistened with just a little of the broth, sprinkled with grated mature cheese and pepper to bring out their goodness. We love these tasty morsels; just writing about them makes my mouth water."

juice of 1 lemon
6 small globe artichokes
3 tbsp extra virgin olive oil
1 small onion, chopped
90 g/3 oz prosciutto, chopped
120 ml/4 fl oz dry white wine
300 g/10 oz shelled fresh peas
salt and pepper
1 tbsp chopped parsley

STIR THE LEMON JUICE INTO A BOWL OF COLD WATER Remove the tough outer leaves from the artichokes and cut off the sharp spikes. Cut the artichokes into wedges lengthwise and immediately drop them into the lemon water to prevent discoloration. The stalks of young artichokes are delicious but they must be scraped well with a vegetable peeler as the outside is bitter. Slice the stalks and add them to the artichokes.

In a large wide pan heat the oil. Add the onion and prosciutto and sauté gently over moderate heat until translucent. Drain the artichokes and add them to the pan. Pour in the wine. Cover and cook over low heat for about 10 minutes. Add the peas and season to taste with salt and pepper. Cook for a further 10 minutes.

Sprinkle with the parsley, transfer to a warm serving dish and serve.

CHINESE DISH WITH ARTICHOKES, A ROSE AND STRAWBERRIES

A Renaissance Extravaganza
by
Piero di Marco PARENTI

AN ACCOUNT OF THE WEDDING OF LORENZO DI PIERO DI COSIMO TO CLARICE ORSINI, ON 4TH JUNE 1469.

THE ORDER OBSERVED IN SERVING WAS MARVELLOUS. For all the dishes were brought in at the door opening into the street, preceded, as is the custom, by trumpets. The like order was observed in taking away the dishes, and each man knew his service and his place and did nought else. The dishes were according to the tables, and among those who brought them in were stewards, each of whom directed his own men to the proper table. There were fifty large dishes, the contents of each of which were sufficient to fill two trenchers, and one trencher was placed between every two guests, a carver being in attendance.

The banquets were prepared for a marriage rather than for a magnificent feast, and I think this was done *de industria* as an example to others not to exceed the modesty and simplicity suitable to marriages, so there was never more than one roast.

In the morning, a small dish, then some boiled meat, then a roast, after that wafers, marzipan and sugared almonds and pine-seeds, then jars of preserved pine-seeds and sweetmeats. In the evening jelly, a roast, fritters, wafers, almonds, and jars of sweetmeats. On Tuesday morning, instead of the roast were sweet pies of succulent vegetables on trenchers; the wines were excellent malvasy, trebbiano, [1] and red wine. Of silver plate there was little.

No sideboards had been placed for the silver. Only tall tables in the middle of the courtyard, round that handsome column on which stands the David, [2] covered with tablecloths, and at the four corners were four great copper basins for the glasses, and behind the tables stood men to hand wine or water to those who served the guests. The same arrangement was made in the garden round the fountain you know. On the tables were silver vessels in which the glasses were put to be kept cool. The salt-cellars, forks, knife-handles, bowls for the fritters, almonds, sugar-plums, and the jars for preserved pine-seeds were of silver; there was none other for the guests save the basins and jugs for washing of hands. The tablecloths were of the finest white damask linen [3] laid according to our fashion.

On Monday morning to all who had received veal, jelly was given, and then about 1500 trenchers full were presented to others. Many religious [monks and nuns] also received gifts of fowls, fish, sweetmeats, wine, and similar things.

In the house here, where the marriage feast was, every respectable person who came in was at once taken to the ground-floor hall, out of the large loggia, to refresh himself with fruit, sweetmeats, and white and red wine. The common folk were not invited.

The feasting began in the morning a little before dinner-time, then every one went away to repose. At about the twentieth hour (4 o'clock) they returned and danced until supper-time on the stage outside, which was decorated with tapestries, benches, and forms, and covered in with large curtains of purple, green, and white cloth, embroidered with the arms of the Medici and the Orsini. Every time a company came on to the stage to dance they took refreshments once or twice, according to the time. First came the trumpeters, then a great silver basin, then many smaller ones full of glasses, then small silver jars full of water, then many flasks of trebbiano and then twenty-three silver bowls full of preserved pine-seeds and sweet conserves. To all was given in abundance and all the dishes were emptied; and the same with the flasks of wine. The account has not been made, but from five to ... thousand pounds of sweetmeats and sugar-plums were consumed.

[1] A Tuscan white wine still much prized.

[2] Donatello's David. It was placed in the courtyard of the Palazzo Vecchio after the expulsion of Piero de' Medici in 1494 and is now in the Bargello.

[3] *Tela di Renza*, or *Rensa*, so-called because it came from Rheims in France.

PIERO DI PARENTI, MS STROZZIANA CODEX 574, BIBLIOTECA NAZIONALE, FLORENCE.

A Dish of Peaches, with a Cucumber

Cetrioli alle Noci

CUCUMBERS WITH WALNUTS

"CUCUMBERS ARE GOOD. Because of their coldness, they are served with onions and pepper, or stewed with gooseberries or verjuice. We never use the large yellow ones in salads, as the English do, but only the small, completely green cucumbers."

6 cucumbers
a handful of fresh white breadcrumbs
2 garlic cloves
60 g/2 oz/½ cup shelled walnuts
2 tsp wine vinegar
3 tbsp extra virgin olive oil
salt and pepper

PEEL THE CUCUMBER AND SLICE IT THINLY. PLACE IN a salad bowl.

Soak the breadcrumbs in water, then squeeze them dry and place in a mortar or food processor, together with the garlic and walnuts. Pound or blend until smooth, if necessary adding a little water to make a homogenous cream. Dilute with the vinegar and oil and add salt and pepper to taste.

Pour the sauce over the cucumber and serve.

Cestini di Piselli

BASKETS FILLED WITH FRESH PEAS

"PEAS ARE THE NOBLEST OF VEGETABLES, especially those whose pods are good to eat as well. They are cooked with herbs in both lean and fat dishes. For the latter we simmer them in a good broth until half done, and then finish cooking them with a seasoning of hard bacon fat chopped with a knife or pounded in a mortar to the consistency of butter."

600 ml/1 pint/2 ½ cups milk
salt
150 g/5 oz/scant 1 cup semolina or farina
30 g/1 oz/2 tbsp unsalted butter
2 eggs
180 g/6 oz/1 ½ cups dry breadcrumbs
extra virgin olive oil for deep frying
225 g/8 oz/1 ½ cups cooked green peas

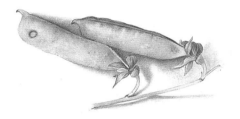

IN A SAUCEPAN BRING THE MILK TO THE BOIL. SEASON with salt and add the semolina in a steady stream while stirring constantly. Cook over low heat for 20 minutes, stirring occasionally. Add half of the butter, stir well and remove from the heat.

Pour the semolina into a bowl and allow to cool. When it is lukewarm stir in 1 egg. Leave to cool completely.

Using your hands, roll the semolina into 6 balls. Make a hollow in the middle of each ball. In a bowl whisk the remaining egg with a pinch of salt. Dip the semolina 'baskets' into the egg, then dredge lightly with breadcrumbs.

Meanwhile, heat the oil to 180°C/350°F in a deep fat fryer. Add the semolina baskets and fry until golden on all sides. Drain well on paper towels.

In a small saucepan melt the rest of the butter. Add the peas and warm them quickly.

Arrange the baskets on a platter. Fill with the warm buttered peas and serve immediately.

A Bowl with Peas and Two Roses

81

Of the State of Tuscanie
by
Sir Robert DALLINGTON

A SURVEY OF THE GREAT DUKES STATE OF TUSCANIE IN THE YEARE OF OUR LORD 1596.

THE OTHER FRUITES OF THESE MOUNTAINES WHICH are indeed use-full and necessary for the sustenance of the inhabitants, are Acornes, Olives, and Chestnuts: of Acornes, especially in the state of *Siena* are very great store, wherewith, over and besides those they eate themselves, they feede their Swine, not having of Beanes or Pease to spare for this purpose; The great Duke maketh yeerely of certaine woods he hath in this State above a thousand Duckets.

They have also Olives, but not in such plentifull manner as to be able to send any Oyle into other parts: for they want hereof to serve their owne turnes; being a commoditie so necessary, as without it, it were not possible they should live, feeding as they doe upon nothing els but cold fruites and rawe herbes, insomuch as the *Villano* and poorer sort feedeth not upon flesh once a moneth, and then most sparingly; as for Butter and Cheese, were it not for *Lombardie* they should scarce know what it meant.

The third benefit of the hils is the Chesnut, the countri-mans bread, as water is his drinke, and except very seldome eateth nothing but those Nuts; the sterility of the countrey being such as not to afford bread of corne for one fourth part of the yeare. It may heere suffice to inferre that the greater part of this State being hilles, and the most of those barraine, & much of these other nothing but Stone: no marvaile then, though they build like the *Agrigentines* and live like the *Scythians*, though they dwell like Princes, & feed like Pesants, though their houses be great and their tables small, though the women have in one day more riches on their back then they spend in three ages on the sustenance of their body. And yet that glory and wealth there is, is in the Cittie, and in the hands of few, to whom all the fruites of the country are conveyed: as for the Artificer he can doe no more but live, whereof scarce one in a citty ever groweth rich, and the poore *Contadines* life is such, as if naturally he were not proud in this extreme miserie, it would move any stranger to pittie his estate.

SIR ROBERT DALLINGTON, 1605.

Vos' Signoria ha Desinato?
by
Fynes MORYSON

OF THE FLORENTINES, THOUGH MOST COURTEOUS, YET sparing, other Italians jeast, saying, that when they meete a man about dinner time, they aske Vos' Signoria ha desinato, Sir, have you dined? and if he answer, I, they replie as if they would have invited him to dinner: but if he answere no, they reply Andate Signor, ch' è otta, Goe Sir, for it is high time to dine. They thinke it best to cherrish and increase friendship by meetings in Market places and Gardens, but hold the table and bed unfit for conversation, where men should come to eate quickly, and sleepe soundly. Thus not provoking appetite with variety of meates, or eating with others for good fellowship, they must needes be more temperate, then others intised by these meanes to eate beyond hunger. In Cities, where many take chambers in one house, they eate at a common table, but each man hath his owne meat provided, the Hostesse dressing it, and serving each man with his owne napkin, glasse, forke, spoone, knife, and ingestar or glasse of wine, which after meate are severally and neately laid up by the Hostesse. And at the table, perhaps one man hath a hen, another a piece of flesh, the third potched egges, and each man severall meat after his diet: but it is no courtesie for one to offer another part of his meate, which they rather take to be done in pride, as if he thought that he had a sallet or egges, could not have a hen or flesh if hee listed for want of money. To conclude, they hold it no honour or disgrace to live plentifully or sparingly, so they live of their owne, and be not in debt, for in that case they are esteemed slaves. Thus living of their owne, they give due honour to superiours, so they returne due respect to them, otherwise they dispise him that is richer, saying in scorne, Let him dine twise a day, and weare two gounes if he will, it is enough for mee to have convenient diet and apparrell. They have a very delicate sauce for rosted meates, called Savore, made of slices of bread, steeped in broath, with as many Walnuts, and some few leaves of Marjoram, beaten in a morter, and mingled therewith, together with the juyce of Gooseberries.

AN ITINERARY, FYNES MORYSON, 1605–17.

Uva e Cipolline

SMALL ONIONS WITH GRAPES

"WHEN THERE ARE NO SPRING ONIONS, we make a salad of roasted onions seasoned with crushed pepper. This is tastier and more wholesome than eating them boiled.

Onions without pepper are excellent for clearing up the sort of bad cough that lingers after a cold."

900 g/2 lb small button (pearl) onions
30 g/1 oz/2 tbsp butter
salt and pepper
90 ml/3 fl oz dry white wine
300 g/10 oz white seedless grapes

BRING A SAUCEPAN OF SALTED WATER TO THE BOIL. Add the onions and blanch for about 5 minutes. Drain and peel.

Melt the butter in the saucepan. Add the onions and season with salt and pepper. Add a little of the wine. Cover the pan and cook over low heat for about 30 minutes, gradually adding the remaining wine as it evaporates.

Add the grapes and, shaking the pan frequently, cook for a further 5 minutes. Arrange on a warm platter and serve at once.

GRAPES WITH PEARS AND A SNAIL

85

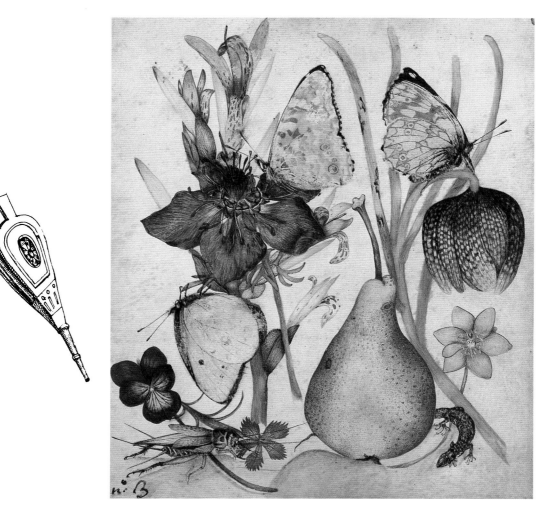

FLOWERS WITH A PEAR, BUTTERFLIES, LIZARD AND A CRICKET

La Festa del Grillo
by
Giuseppe CONTI

ON THE MORNING OF THE ASCENSION, A LITTLE AFTER dawn, the first bands began to appear with the baskets or the panniers with bottles of wine and dishes, glasses and plates, who made their way slowly out towards Cascine. There was a great deal of hubbub everywhere on the road but it was the people with the wicker traps for the crickets who made more racket than anyone else. Fathers gave the crickets to their children, and in the evening they put the cage of millet stalks outside the windows, to the great discomfiture of tenants who were quite unable to sleep.

Around five, as soon as the sun was up, the crowd became denser, and everybody went to Neri's, to drink milk fresh from the cow. This was the tradition for those wishing to celebrate the Ascension in the proper manner. Everyone scattered along woodland paths and into woods known as "gli Alberini", to find a shady place to cook lunch in the open air, and enjoy a meal upon the grass. Meanwhile, woodsmoke began to appear, from fires being lit to prepare the roasts, and there was a smell in the air of lamb being cooked with peas in the small ovens, brought along in baskets by those who made their own improvised *trattorie*.

From the Prato Gate all the way to the *Palazzo*, one could see tables ready laid. Each of these *trattorie*, had five or six earthenware ovens to cook the lamb which on that day was eaten as a blessing, from great earthenware dishes, called *"di Cancelli"*, and on the benches stood pyramids of bottles of wine and vermouth and white wine; and salami, ham and hard-boiled eggs, and rings of fresh, crispy, homemade bread, enough to make the mouth water, even for those who had no appetite. Then a vast number of mixed grills, and chickens on spits, turning before flames glowing red as if from the sun's rays, which made it all a great pleasure. Those who had brought their own snacks or lunches, sat down on the grass, and at eight o'clock they began eating salami, mortadella and boiled eggs, and to drink glasses of wine, to laugh and make a lot of noise as if they were in another world.

FIRENZE VECCHIA, GIUSEPPE CONTI, 1899.

Of Florentine Everyday Life
by
Giuseppe CONTI

IT COULD BE SAID THAT EATING-HABITS WERE MORE OR less the same in all the households. In the morning, for breakfast instead of coffee with milk as is the custom today, *pappa* (a kind of porridge, in fact) was prepared in the saucepan; it often had a smoky taste because a wood fire was made which was lit with shavings. The children were sent to school with a lunch-basket, which consisted only of a slice of bread with butter, or a dried fig, or an apple, or a dozen or so beans, a bunch of cherries or a slice of polenta, depending on the season. When the bell rang, they all returned home to lunch, and the workshops did not reopen between one and three. The frugal meal usually consisted of soup or boiled meat; on feast-days the favourite dish was offal in casserole, liver with egg, chicken in the *bastardella* (stewpot) or lamb. For carnival, roast pork rib was much in favour, and the children turned the spit with the cord, competing for whose turn it was; the mothers often awarded it to the best-behaved, as a sort of reward. In the evening supper (dinner) was around eight, in summer and winter alike; but they waited for the head of the household to return from his workshop, bringing with him, as an extra, the *affettato*, slices of salami or ham or more often mortadella, which was also called *gnocchiona*, and was the cheapest of all the cooked meats. In Lent caviar was eaten; it was served in slices in those days and was delicious; otherwise herring or dried figs, nuts and dried apples: in short everything that could be bought cheaply and could be eaten with a slice of bread.

The wine in those good old days cost four or five crazie a bottle, and if it was old, seven crazie – about fifty centesimos! When the time of the vintage came, if the year had been a good one, the wine cost almost nothing. So much so, that there were exceptional years in which the people went to the convent of the nuns of St Mary Magdalene, or the Maglio or Santa Verdiana and others, with certain bottles which seemed like barrels, and filled them for one crazia – about ten centesimi.

FIRENZE VECCHIA, GIUSEPPE CONTI, 1899.

88

A Dish with Cherries and Carnations

A Dish of Grapes, with a Peach

90

Sorbetto di Uva

GRAPE SORBET

"AT THE BEGINNING OF JULY the *luglienga* grapes, named after the month, are ready to eat. Although not the best in the world, they are somewhat over-esteemed for being the first to ripen. These grapes are quite harmless, unlike some others. Since they are rather weak, we do not make much wine out of them; in fact most of them get eaten anyway."

1.5 kg/3 lb red grapes
240 ml/8 fl oz water
120 g/4 oz sugar
3 tbsp lemon juice
1 egg white

GENTLY SIMMER THE GRAPES WITH THE WATER AND sugar for 10 minutes until soft. Pass through a food mill into a bowl and set the bowl in a larger bowl of iced water to cool.

Add the lemon juice. Still-freeze in a shallow container or in an ice cream machine. When frozen, break into chunks, put in a food processor with the egg white and blend until creamy. Freeze again until firm and serve.

91

Schiacciata con L'Uva

FLORENTINE FLAT BREAD WITH GRAPES

"I HAVE SAID NOTHING YET about the enormous quantities of grapes that we hang from the rafters, or keep fresh all winter in large boxes of new straw, not to mention the even larger amounts of raisins we dry in the sun or in ovens."

2 tbsp fresh yeast, or 15 g/½ oz dry yeast
150 ml/5 fl oz lukewarm milk
300 g/10 oz flour
130 g/4 ½ oz/10 tbsp sugar
pinch of salt
500 g/1 lb 2 oz black grapes, pitted, skin on
200 g/7 oz raisins soaked in Vin Santo or other sweet dessert wine

DISSOLVE THE FRESH YEAST IN THE LUKEWARM MILK. (If using dry yeast, add to the dry ingredients, leaving milk to the end.) Mound the flour in a large bowl and make a well in the centre. Add all but 2 tbsp of the sugar and the salt and stir in the yeast mixture. Knead for 5 minutes, then cover with a clean cloth and leave in a warm place to rise until double the original size.

Punch down to remove the air and shape into two rounds about 20 cm/8 inches across. Place one on a floured baking sheet and cover with half the grapes and half the drained raisins.

Cover with the second round of dough and on top put the rest of the grapes and raisins. Leave, covered, to rise again until doubled in size.

Sprinkle with the reserved sugar and bake in a pre-heated 180°C/350°F/gas 4 oven for about 45 minutes.

A Dish with Melon, and a Slice of Watermelon

93

Fichi Secchi al Porto

DRIED FIGS IN PORT

"DRIED FIGS, ROASTED A LITTLE and eaten at bedtime, will help to clear up those nasty coughs that linger after a bad cold. But make sure the figs are not stale."

18 dried figs
240 ml/8 fl oz port
a handful of fresh mint leaves
240 ml/8 fl oz whipping cream

LEAVE THE FIGS TO SOAK IN THE PORT FOR AT LEAST 24 hours.
Drain the figs and make a small incision in the side of each one. Into each cut, insert a mint leaf. Whip the cream. Place the figs on a plate and serve, with the cream.

A Dish with Figs, Fig Leaves and Two Small Pomegranates

Il Giuoco del Calcio
by
Richard LASSELS

IN WINTER THEIR *Giuoco del Calcio* (a play something like our football, but that they play with their hands) happens every night from Epiphany till Lent, with their Principi di Calcio. This being a thing particular to Florence, deserves to be described. The two factions of the Calcio, the Red, and the Green, choose each of them a Prince, some young Cavalier of a good purse. These Princes being chosen, choose a world of Officers, and lodge in some great pallace, where they keep their courts, receive Embassadors from one another, and give them publik audience in state. During these serious treatyes which last for many nights the Secretaryes of State (two prime witts) read before their several Princes bills for regulating and reforming the abuses of their subjects; and read openly petitions and secret advises. In fine, having spunn out thus the time till neare Carnevale, or shoftide, the two Princes resolve on a battle at Calcio. Upon the day apointed, the two Princes of the Calcio come in a most stately Cavalcata with all the yong noblemen and gentlemen of the towne, upon the best horses they can finde, with scarfs, red, or green, about their Armes. Haveing made their several Cavalcatas before the Great Dukes throne or scaffold, they light from their horses, and enter into the lists with trompets sounding before them, accompanyed with a stately train, with their combatants in their several liveryes. Having rancked themselves a pretty distance one from the other, their standard bearers at sound of trumpet, carry both at once, their standards to the foot of the Great Dukes scaffold. This done, the Ball is throwne up in the midst between them, and to it they go with great nimbleness, sleight, and discretion. All animosites arriseing here, end here too. At last, that side which throwes, or strikes the Ball over the rayles of the other side, winns the day, and runns to the standards, which they carry away till night, at what time the conquering Prince enterteins them at a Festino di Ballo at Court, made to some Lady; and where all his chief Officers and combatants dance alone with the Ladyes at the Ball.

THE VOYAGE OF ITALY, RICHARD LASSELS, 1670.

The Festa del Calcio

A Dish of Small Pears, with Medlars and Cherries

Crostata di Pere al Cioccolato

CHOCOLATE PEAR TART

"EARLY IN THE SUMMER come muscat pears, which also grow in England, but do not ripen so early. Although they are a small fruit, everyone likes them because of their musky scent, hence the names *muscardini, muscatelli.*"

120 g/4 oz/1 stick butter, softened
200 g/7 oz/scant 1 ½ cups flour
1 egg
120 g/4 oz/scant ½ cup fine sugar
50 g/1 ¾ oz/½ cup cocoa powder
2 ½ tbsp orange marmalade
2 pears
CHOCOLATE FILLING:
100 g/3 ½ oz bitter chocolate
60 g/2 oz/4 tbsp butter
2 eggs, separated
100 g/3 ½ oz/½ cup fine sugar

MAKE A DOUGH WITH THE BUTTER, FLOUR, EGG, SUGAR and cocoa.

Line a 20 cm/8 inch tart pan with the dough and cover the bottom with the marmalade.

Peel the pears, cut into quarters and remove the cores. Arrange them in the dough case.

To make the filling, melt the chocolate and butter over low heat, then set aside to cool. Beat the egg whites until stiff. Beat together the yolks and sugar until pale and fluffy. Add the chocolate mixture and fold in the egg whites. Pour the mixture over the pears and bake in a preheated 180°C/350°F/gas 4 oven for about 40 minutes.

Crostata di Fichi e Limoni

FRESH FIG AND LEMON TART

"TOWARDS THE END OF MAY the 'flower figs' are good. These early, or first-crop, figs are so called because this noble tree produces, instead of flowers, a fruit even bigger than the real fruit which it bears in early September, and which I shall describe later on. In Venice they call this the Madonna fig, for no good reason that I can think of."

200 g/7 oz/1 ½ cups flour
1 egg yolk
225 g/8 oz/1 ¼ cups fine sugar
100 g/3 ½ oz/7 tbsp butter, softened
6 lemons
1 kg/2 ¼ lb fresh figs, washed, skins left on
1 tsp fennel seeds

PUT THE FLOUR IN A MOUND ON THE WORKING SURFACE. Make a well in the centre and add the egg yolk, half the sugar and the butter. Blend together to make a dough. Perforate the skins of the lemons all over with a fork, then boil them in water for a couple of minutes. Repeat the boiling process 3 times, changing the water each time. Drain and slice finely, leaving on the skins. Put the lemon slices in a saucepan with the remaining sugar and half a glass of water.

Cover and cook over low heat for about 10 minutes. Drain off the syrup and reserve.

Roll out the dough and use to line a buttered and floured tart pan with a removable bottom. Cover the dough with the lemon slices. Slice the figs and arrange on top. Pour the lemon syrup over the figs, sprinkle with the fennel seeds and bake in a preheated 180°C/350°F/gas 4 oven for about 45 minutes. Cool, then remove from the pan and serve on a platter.

CHINESE BOWL WITH FIGS, CHERRIES AND A GOLDFINCH

101

Of Local Produce
by
Fynes MORYSON

IN THE UPPER PART OF ITALY, THEY PLANT IN ONE AND the same field, Olive and Almond trees, and under them sow Corne, and in the furrowes plant Vines, which shoote up, resting uppon short stakes, and yeeld strong wine of divers sorts, because they grow not high, and the ground being hilly, hath more benefit from the Sunne beating upon it. The soyle of Toscany being hilly and stony, seemed to me at the first sight to be barren, but after I found it not onely to yeeld fruites plentifully, but also good increase of Corne, as of one measure sowed, commonly eight or ten measures, often fourteene, and sometimes twenty five; neither doe they give the ground rest by laying it fallow, as we doe, but each second yeere they sow part of it with Beanes and Pulse, yeelding plentiful increase, and then burying the stubble to rot in the ground, make it thereby fat to beare wheate againe. My selfe observed, that at the foot of the South-side of the Alpes, they gather Wheate and Rie in the moneth of June, and then sow the same fields with lighter kinds of Graine, which they gather in the moneth of October: yet by reason of the multitude of the people, and the narrownesse of the Land, the Italians not onely carry not any grane into forraigne parts, but also the Merchants bringing grane to them, are cherished by the Princes, with faire words and rewards, that they may come againe, more specially by the Duke of Florence, who takes care to provide for his Countrey, not onely grane from Sicily and all other parts, but also sheepe out of Lombardy, which he divides among his Subjects, at what price he list, taking this charge upon him to see that his people want not victuals, as wel for the publike good, as his owne great gaine.

AN ITINERARY, FYNES MORYSON, 1605–17

A Slice of Melon

Salsa di Fragole

STRAWBERRY SAUCE

"IN ITALY, it is only in spring that we have these fragrant and health-giving berries, whereas you happy mortals, though you do not get them so early, have them twice a year, in mid June and in October. Last year I was in Cambridge on 28 October, and was amazed to be eating strawberries by the plateful, not just one or two. They were exquisite."

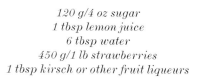

120 g/4 oz sugar
1 tbsp lemon juice
6 tbsp water
450 g/1 lb strawberries
1 tbsp kirsch or other fruit liqueurs

IN A SAUCEPAN COMBINE THE SUGAR, LEMON JUICE AND water. Bring to the boil over low heat and boil until the syrup coats a spoon, about 5 minutes.

In a blender combine the strawberries, syrup and kirsch. Blend until a creamy sauce is formed. Allow to cool before serving. Redcurrants, raspberries, pears and peaches can be substituted for strawberries in this sauce, to accompany desserts such as sliced raw fruit or cooked fruits, or ice cream.

Blue Bowl with Strawberries, Pears and a Grasshopper

Dog with Sweet Biscuits and a Cup

Biscotti alle Mandorle

ALMOND COOKIES

"ALMOND PASTE IS MADE into all kinds of delicious and wholesome confections, as well as marzipan, most of which are quite common here. Not so well known, however, are almond and bread soup, almond milk and almond butter."

270 g/9 oz/scant 2 cups flour
180 g/6 oz/scant 1 cup fine sugar
1 tsp baking powder
2 eggs
1 egg yolk
120 g/4 oz/scant 1 cup unblanched almonds, roughly chopped

MIX THE FLOUR, SUGAR, BAKING POWDER, EGGS AND yolk together well by hand or in a food processor. Add the almonds and knead briefly. Divide the dough into 6 parts and form each into a fat cigar shape. Bake in a preheated oven 180°C/350°F/gas 4 oven for about 20 minutes.

Take them out of the oven. Cut them across into 5 cm/2 inch pieces and replace in the oven to bake for a further 10 minutes, until golden.

Cool before serving.

ACKNOWLEDGEMENTS

The publishers and compilers wish to extend particular thanks to the following for their kind help and advice in the preparation of this anthology:

Gerardo Casale, author of the monograph *Giovanna Garzoni* (Jandi Sapi Editori, Rome, 1991); Angela Cipriani, of the Accademia di San Luca, Rome, for permission to reproduce Garzoni's paintings from their collection; FMR Magazine, for photographs kindly loaned; Index, Florence (Ancilla Antonini) and photographer Paolo Tosi for arranging photography in Florence; Silvia Meloni, Director of Research at the Soprintendenza Per I Beni Artistici e Storici, Florence, whose article on Garzoni in *FMR* in 1983 first brought her to our attention, and for permission to reproduce the paintings in the Galleria Palatina, in the Pitti Palace, and from the Gabinetto dei Disegni e delle Stampe, in the Uffizi.

PICTURE ACKNOWLEDGEMENTS
Accademia di San Luca, Rome : 7
Accademia di San Luca, Biblioteca Sarti, Rome: 5 (min. 18), 10, 12 (min. 19), 20 (min. 17), 27 (min. 21), 59 (min. 22), 80L (min. 5), 86 (min. 3), 103 (min. 20)
Cleveland Museum of Art, USA, bequest of Elma M. Schniewind, in memory of her parents, Mr and Mrs Frank Geib, 55. 140 : 6
Fotomas Index : 42
Galleria Palatina, Florence/FMR, Milan ; 19 (inv. 1890/4771), 29 (inv. 1890/4766), 45 (inv. 1890/4761), 75 (inv. 1890/4760), 81 (inv. 1890/4762), 85 (inv. 1890/4769), 105 (inv. 1890/4758), 106 (1890/4770)
Galleria Palatina, Florence/Paolo Tosi : 22 (inv. 1890/4749), 35 (inv. 1890/4759), 40 (inv. 1890/4751), 49 (inv. 1890/4757), 53 (inv. 1890/4778), 57 (inv. 1890/4747), 67 (inv. 1890/4779), 71 (inv. 1890/4765), 78 (inv.

1890/4763), 89 (inv. 1890/4764), 90 (inv. 1890/4748), 93 (inv. 1890/4777), 95 (inv. 1890/4767), 98 (inv. 1890/4772), 101 (inv. 1890/4750)
Galleria degli Uffizi, Gabinetto dei Disegni e delle Stampe/FMR, Milan: 62 (Inv. 1890/4782)
Galleria degli Uffizi, Gabinetto dei Disegni e delle Stampe/Paolo Tosi: 23 (249 ORN), 28 (2150 ORN), 50 (inv. 1890/4780), 74 (detail) (2147 ORN), 80R (detail) (2148 ORN)
Lodi Collection, Campione d'Italia/FMR, Milan : 25, 32

PRIVATE COLLECTIONS:
from Vedute delle principale contrade, piazze . . . di Firenze G. Zocchi, 1744 : 15, 39, 46, 60, 65, 97
from Musica, Ballo e drammatica all corte Mediceo dal 1600 al 1637 Antonio Solerti : 31
from Opera Bartolomeo Scappi, 1570 : 73

TEXT ACKNOWLEDGEMENTS
Especial thanks are due to Gillian Riley, translator of *The Fruits, Herbs and Vegetables of Italy* by Giacomo Castelvetro (Viking, 1989) for permission to reprint the extracts from her translation of his 1614 manuscript which form the recipe introductions.

Translations from Giuseppe Conti *Firenze Vecchia,* 1899 pps 37, 61, 64, 87, 88 and Conti's *Fatti e Anedotti di Storia Fiorentina,* 1902 pps 72–3 are by Brian Williams, of Rome. The Parenti extract on pages 76–77 is from *Lives of the Early Medici as told in their Correspondence* translated by Janet Ross, 1910. Thanks are also due to the following for their assistance in research: Norma Macmillan, Clare Malim, Sally Tomsett, Lisa Zeitz.

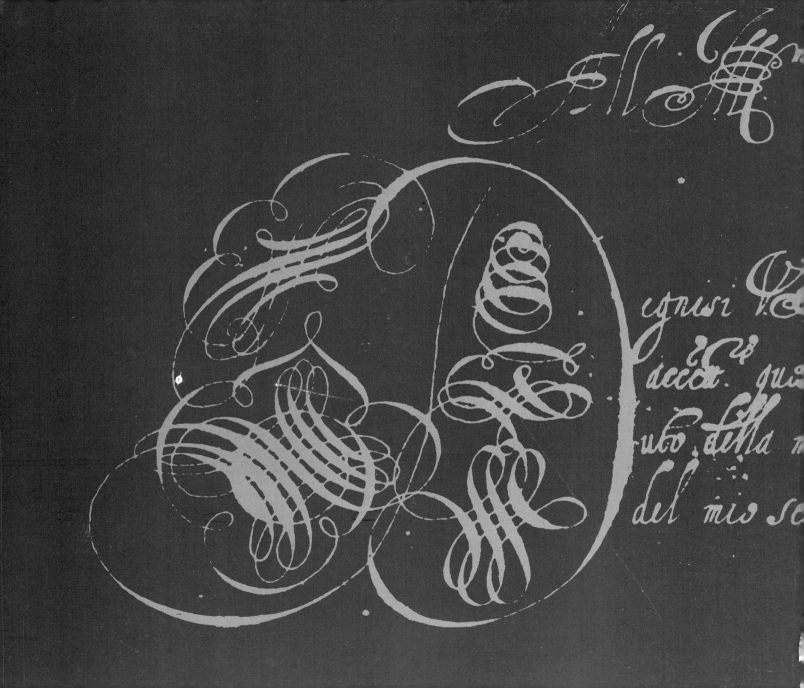